# Faith

## STUDY GUIDE

## CHUCK SMITH

THE WORD
FOR TODAY

P.O. Box 8000, Costa Mesa, CA 92628 • (800) 272-9673 • www.twft.com • info@twft.com

This study guide has been designed to be used to accompany the book *Faith* written by Chuck Smith. It is highly recommended for Bible studies relating to new believer fellowships and discipleship ministries. It's advisable to discuss the answers within a group setting, learn from one another, and consider any prayer requests verbalized.

Each question can be answered by referring to the text *Faith* and by reading the scriptural references stated within this study guide.

THE WORD
FOR TODAY

Published by The Word For Today
P.O. Box 8000, Costa Mesa, CA 92628
www.twft.com
(800) 272-WORD (9673)
© 2010 The Word For Today
ISBN: 978-1-59751-098-1

All rights reserved. No part of this publication may be reproduced, stored in a retrieval system, or transmitted in any form or by any means without the express written consent of The Word For Today Publishers.

Unless otherwise indicated, Scripture quotations in this book are taken from the New King James Version of the Bible. Copyright © 1979, 1980, 1982, by Thomas Nelson, Inc., Publishers. Used by permission. Translational emendations, amplifications, and paraphrases are by the author.

Printed in the United States of America.

# CONTENTS

### PART ONE
## The Nature of Faith

1. What Is Faith? ..................................................... 5
2. How Does Faith Operate? ........................................ 8
3. What Does Faith Accomplish? ................................. 11
4. What Most Pleases God? ....................................... 14
5. A Faith That Works ............................................ 17
6. The Marvel of Unbelief ........................................ 20
7. The Triumph of Faith .......................................... 23

### PART TWO
## The Look of Faith

8. Abraham: Man of Faith ........................................ 26
9. Isaac: Son of Faith ............................................ 29
10. Ruth: Adventure of Faith .................................... 32
11. Mary: Obedience of Faith ................................... 35
12. Paul: Apostle of Faith ....................................... 38
13. Peter: From Doubt to Faith ................................. 41
14. The Soldier & the Mother: Great Faith .................... 44

### PART THREE
## The Walk of Faith

15. Living by Faith in a Faithful God .......................... 47
16. How Can I Pray in Faith? ................................... 50
17. How Can I Step Out in Faith? .............................. 53
18. How Can I Stand Firm in Faith? ........................... 56
19. How Can I Pass Tests of Faith? ............................ 59
20. How Can I Grow in Faith? ................................... 62

Before you begin
your study in *Faith*, take a
moment and prayerfully consider
why the Lord has placed this study in
your hands today.

Write a prayer seeking the Holy Spirit's
guidance and leading as you read and
apply these lessons.

_____

_____

_____

_____

_____

Date: _____

# PART ONE

# The Nature of Faith

# What Is Faith?

Read Chapter 1, *What Is Faith?*

1. Write your personal definition of faith. Next, write the biblical interpretation of faith according to Hebrews 11:1.

_____

_____

_____

_____

2. There is abundant evidence for the existence of God all around you. List some evidences for the existence of God in your life today.

_____     _____

_____     _____

_____     _____

_____     _____

3. By faith, the author of Hebrews reveals the nature of God. He proclaimed that God spoke all things, both seen and unseen, into existence. Meditate on this kind of faith as you copy Hebrews 11:3 here.

_____

_____

_____

_____

4. There are various ways people define God. How do you describe God?

_____

_____

_____

_____

5. Record Hebrews 11:6 and commit it to memory.

_____

_____

_____

_____

6. Satan will always contradict what God has said. Faith believes in God and His promises rather than listens to the opposition of the enemy. Write a prayer using Scripture of how you are choosing to believe God's promises by faith.

_____

_____

_____

_____

7. You are able to base your faith on the promises of God because He is always true to His Word. What truth do you learn about God from Hebrews 6:18?

_____

_____

_____

_____

_____

8. Sometimes we can become frustrated when we don't understand what God is doing. Whenever you are faced with doubt or confusion, what is the Lord's answer to you in Habakkuk 2:4?

_____

_____

_____

9. Ephesians 2:8 states that salvation is a free gift received by grace through faith. Define grace based upon what it means to you presently and how it has affected your life in the past.

_____

_____

_____

_____

10. We see many examples today of men and women whom the Lord prepared for the life of faith. Expound upon some ways the Lord has been preparing you to live by faith.

_____

_____

_____

_____

# How Does Faith Operate?

Read Chapter 2, *How Does Faith Operate?*

1.  Outline the four keys to Abraham's faith as noted in Romans 4:19-21.

    _____

    _____

    _____

    _____

2.  We may think that if something is difficult for us, it must be difficult for God. When King Asa was outnumbered, summarize his declaration of faith found in 2 Chronicles 14:11.

    _____

    _____

    _____

    _____

3. Your human limitations can at times stand in the way of your faith. Write Luke 18:27 here and commit it to memory.

_____

_____

4. It is essential to stand upon the promises of God and not stagger. Refer to the following Scriptures and describe how your faith can operate by standing on the promise given.

Matthew 11:28 _____

_____

Philippians 4:7, 19 _____

_____

_____

5. List several people in your life who may be staggering at the promises of God and pray for them.

_____     _____

_____     _____

_____     _____

6. A true depiction of faith is rejoicing before there is any evidence of the fulfillment of God's promises. How can this faith be exemplified in you today?

_____

_____

_____

7. You may divide your devotion between God's Word and man's word when situations look hopeless, but man can never assure you of peace. Use Psalm 118:8 to support this statement.

_____

_____

8.  It may be easy for you to believe that God exists, yet having faith—whatever may happen—is a daily commitment. Read Jeremiah 32:17 and explain why you can have confidence that God can handle anything you may face.

_____

_____

_____

_____

9.  After studying this chapter, what are some ways you can completely surrender your life and begin putting your faith wholly in the Lord and not in man? What obstacles are preventing you from doing this?

_____

_____

_____

_____

_____

10. Many years ago when Calvary Chapel was experiencing tremendous growth and had to expand, the Lord provided everything it needed. As a result, God received the credit and glory—not man. Write a prayer asking that the Lord's will be done and not your own—in order to give Him the glory.

_____

_____

_____

_____

_____

# What Does Faith Accomplish?

Read Chapter 3, *What Does Faith Accomplish?*

1.  You can rest in the Lord even when you don't know how or when God will work out the circumstances. List the worries you have in your life and surrender them to God.

   _____     _____
   _____     _____
   _____     _____
   _____     _____

2.  Faith is not a means to gain material goods. Jesus revealed the potential of faith to His disciples in Matthew 17:20. In order to attain this faith, what constitutes discipleship according to Matthew 16:24?

   _____
   _____
   _____
   _____

3. Hebrews chapter 11 details what these believers accomplished through faith. Share what comes to mind as you read these achievements.

_____

_____

_____

_____

4. There may be times when faith won't always deliver you from adverse circumstances. What extraordinary promise does the Lord provide in Isaiah 43:2?

_____

_____

_____

_____

5. Faith is a means by which God can accomplish His purposes through your life. What surprising truth do you learn about God's will in 1 Peter 4:19?

_____

_____

_____

_____

6. Have you ever given a problem to the Lord only to take it right back? First Peter 5:7 exhorts us to "cast all your care upon Him, for He cares for you." What does 2 Timothy 1:12 add to this?

_____

_____

_____

_____

7.  In Mark 5, two desperate people discovered the huge potential of faith. Describe their different approaches to Jesus and what their faith accomplished.

_____

_____

_____

_____

8.  The Lord is waiting for you to come to Him in faith to receive His touch of healing. Memorize Philippians 4:6-7 and write down the exhortations from verse 6 and the assurance from verse 7.

_____

_____

_____

_____

_____

9.  When you place your faith in Jesus, He does not see you in your sinful state, but rather in your perfected state. Meditate on Jude 1:24 and note your thoughts.

_____

_____

_____

_____

10. God loves you and desires to accomplish amazing things in your life. Write a prayer of surrender and thanks to Him, and ask Him by faith to accomplish His will in you.

_____

_____

_____

_____

# What Most Pleases God?

Read Chapter 4, *What Most Pleases God?*

1.  If given the choice, you would probably much rather please God than displease Him. What do you learn from Hebrews 11:6 that pleases Him?

    _____

    _____

    _____

    _____

2.  Since faith and trust in God pleases His heart, what type of attitude do you think displeases Him? Name as many characteristics as you can that are displeasing to God.

    _____    _____

    _____    _____

    _____    _____

    _____    _____

    _____    _____

3. The Lord created you for one purpose—to bring Him pleasure—and you'll never be satisfied until you fulfill that purpose. Meditate on Revelation 4:11 as you copy it here.

_____
_____
_____
_____

4. Faith so pleases the Lord that He rewards you just for having it. Read 2 Timothy 4:7-8 and James 1:12 and write a response of praise to the Lord for His promises of blessing when you trust in Him.

_____
_____
_____
_____

5. Because Abraham's faith pleased God, the Lord said to him, "I am your exceedingly great reward" (Genesis 15:1). Do you feel rich because you have Jesus? List some ways you feel blessed by God simply because of your faith in Him.

_____     _____
_____     _____
_____     _____
_____     _____
_____     _____

6. In Romans 4, Paul explains that Abraham was justified (he pleased God) by faith—not by works. Your good works here on earth will not get you a ticket to heaven. What is your response to this statement?

_____
_____
_____
_____

7. Salvation is the greatest reward of all. How much faith is required for you to be saved and to receive the greatest reward possible? Refer to Matthew 17:20 for your answer.

_____

_____

_____

_____

8. True faith that pleases the Lord isn't simply believing that there is a God. Explore what Romans 10:9 says and explain what kind of saving faith pleases God.

_____

_____

_____

_____

9. Read Hebrews 6:12. God loves the kind of faith that works patiently without growing sluggish. What does Galatians 6:9 add to this?

_____

_____

_____

_____

10. Faith pleases the Lord and He loves to bless His children. Write a prayer thanking God for accepting you as you are, and pray that you may have faith that pleases Him.

_____

_____

_____

_____

_____

# A Faith That Works

Read Chapter 5, *A Faith That Works.*

1.  To profess one thing and then do the opposite is a lie. Research what
    1 John 2:3-4 says about the evidence of true faith.

    _____

    _____

    _____

    _____

2.  It is vital to understand that you are saved by grace through faith—not
    by works. Read these Scriptures and clarify what the apostle Paul means
    when he writes about grace and "the work of faith."

Ephesians 2:8-9 _____

    _____

1 Thessalonians 1:3 _____

    _____

    _____

3. Some believe there is a contradiction between what Paul and James teach regarding faith and works. Study James 2:14, 17-18 and explain the relationship between faith and works.

_____

_____

_____

_____

4. Read 1 Corinthians 15:10. Paul shares how the grace of God in his life provoked him to greater labor. Share some ways in which your faith in God's grace is working in your life today.

_____    _____

_____    _____

_____    _____

_____    _____

5. When you declare that Jesus is your Lord, it signifies that you are His servant. After looking over Luke 17:7-10, what should be your state of mind toward whatever you do for the Lord?

_____

_____

_____

_____

6. Read the parable found in Matthew 25:14-30. What does Jesus teach regarding the lord's accounting of what the master entrusts to his servants?

_____

_____

_____

_____

7. Just like the servants in the Matthew 25 parable, you too will stand before the Lord to give an account. What has God entrusted to you, and what will you be able to present to Him?

_____    _____

_____    _____

_____    _____

_____    _____

_____    _____

8. James testifies how Rahab the harlot was justified by her works. According to Hebrews 11:31 and James 2:25, what constituted Rahab's work of faith?

_____

_____

_____

_____

9. Genuine faith will always reveal itself through works of faith. Write out James 2:26 and meditate on this truth.

_____

_____

_____

_____

10. Faith and works are like two oars on a rowboat—both are needed. Jesus said, "You will know them by their fruits" (Matthew 7:16). Take a moment to reflect on what kind of fruit your life is producing and expound upon what the Lord reveals to you.

_____

_____

_____

_____

# The Marvel of Unbelief

Read Chapter 6, *The Marvel of Unbelief.*

1.  Sometimes if things don't go as planned, people tend to grumble and complain. This stems from unbelief—not trusting that God has a better plan. Read Isaiah 55:8-9, and write what you discover about your plans as compared with God's.

    _____

    _____

    _____

    _____

2.  Mark 6:2-3 reveals that the people of Nazareth did not believe in Jesus, even after hearing His teaching and seeing some of His works. What do you think accounted for their unbelief?

    _____

    _____

    _____

    _____

    _____

3. According to John 3:18, what is the consequence of unbelief? What is your reaction to this statement?

_____

_____

_____

_____

4. Although we have the Bible and testimonies of changed lives, why do you think some people do not believe in Jesus today?

_____

_____

_____

_____

5. With so many misconceptions about Jesus, how can you know the truth about Him? Read John 20:31 to assist you with your answer.

_____

_____

_____

_____

6. Mark 6:5-6 gives us this sad statement: "He could do no mighty works there ... and He marveled because of their unbelief." How and why would the Nazarenes' unbelief affect the works of Jesus?

_____

_____

_____

_____

7. Much like the Nazarenes, unbelief can keep you from God's blessings. Are there areas of unbelief in your life today which might be hindering Jesus' work because you don't bring them to Him? Take some time now to lay those at His feet.

_____

_____

_____

_____

8. Many people hold the opinion, "Seeing is believing." Comment on Jesus' response about this in John 20:29.

_____

_____

_____

_____

9. God has offered to you so many glorious promises if you would just believe. As God told Joshua, "Every place where you put your foot, I have given it to you for your possession" (Joshua 1:3). Another promise is declared in 2 Peter 1:4. Write it here and commit it to memory.

_____

_____

_____

_____

10. There comes a point of no return when someone continually rebels against God. After reading John 12:37-40, write a prayer for a friend or loved one who has refused to believe in the grace and love of God.

_____

_____

_____

_____

# The Triumph of Faith

Read Chapter 7, *The Triumph of Faith.*

1.  Is there a situation in your life where you feel you need the triumph of faith? Take some time to focus on the Lord and His power in order to have that victory. Make a request to God here.

    _____

    _____

    _____

    _____

2.  Although Job went through tremendous trials and suffering, he still had a triumph of faith. Read Job 19:25-27 and jot down each victorious phrase that Job acclaims.

    _____

    _____

    _____

    _____

3. It's important to remember in the midst of pain or confusion never to let go of what you do know for something you don't know. After reading Job's statement of faith in the previous question, what can you know for sure?

_____

_____

_____

_____

4. Job was able to experience the triumph of faith because he focused on his Redeemer, his *Goel*. Describe what it means to you that Jesus is your *Goel* (Redeemer).

_____

_____

_____

_____

5. Victory was inevitable in Job's life because he was confident that God was in control of all his circumstances. Summarize his proclamation in Job 1:21.

_____

_____

_____

_____

6. What was Job's response to his wife in Job 2:9-10 when she denounced his unwavering faith? How do you think you would have responded?

_____

_____

_____

_____

7.  In order to triumph in faith, you must stand upon certain foundational truths. Explain what you learn about God from these Scriptures.

Psalm 121:7 _____

Romans 8:31 _____

2 Timothy 1:12 _____

1 John 4:10 _____

8.  While you are enduring trials, you will often find it difficult to obey the Scripture, "Wait on the Lord" (Psalm 27:14). What should you be praying for?

_____

_____

_____

_____

9.  What truth is found in Philippians 4:13 that can help you preprogram victory in your life? Commit this verse to memory.

_____

_____

_____

_____

10. Because you have declared Jesus Christ as your Lord and Savior, God will record your triumphs of faith and He'll bury your failures. Express your gratitude to the Lord for this wonderful promise.

_____

_____

_____

_____

# PART TWO

# The Look of Faith

# Abraham: Man of Faith

Read Chapter 8, *Abraham: Man of Faith.*

1. The three major monotheistic religions of the world—Islam, Judaism and Christianity—all revere the name of Abraham. Yet he wasn't blessed because of his goodness. On what basis does God bestow His blessings?

   _____

   _____

   _____

   _____

2. When God gave Abram instructions to move away from Babylon, He did not give Abram the next step until he completed the first step by faith. Give an example of a time in your life when God led you one step at a time.

   _____

   _____

   _____

   _____

3. Read Genesis 13:10-11. Abram and his nephew, Lot, ran into a problem. Yet because of Abram's strong commitment to God, what was his reaction? What virtue do you learn from Abram?

_____

_____

_____

_____

4. In order for God to bless you, you need to step out in faith and appropriate His promises. Search the Scriptures and cite the references for "trust."

_____

_____

_____

_____

5. The greatest promise of all is the coming of the Messiah. The man of faith, Abraham, believed and was accounted righteous—even though he died without _seeing_ that promise. Read Hebrews 11:13 and share your response.

_____

_____

_____

_____

6. Examine Genesis 17:1-5. God transformed Abram to Abraham by inserting the Spirit, the "H" into his name. Explain the significance of this. Refer to a commentary if needed.

_____

_____

_____

_____

7.  God often allows you to come to the end of yourself in order to get you to a place of hopelessness before He works. Why do you think He does this?

_____

_____

_____

_____

8.  Write Genesis 18:14. What truth do you always need to remember?

_____

_____

_____

_____

9.  When God shows you areas of your flesh that displease Him, what is He seeking to do with you?

_____

_____

_____

_____

10. The New Testament repeatedly uses Abraham as the classic example of a man of faith—without mentioning his failures. Read these Scriptures and list Abraham's examples for us to be faithful.

Romans 4:1-3 _____

Galatians 3:6 _____

Hebrews 11:8 _____

James 2:21, 23 _____

_____

# Isaac: Son of Faith

Read Chapter 9, *Isaac: Son of Faith*.

1.  God established His covenant with Isaac, the son of promise. Write the promise found in Genesis 17:19 and explain how it relates to you today.

   _____

   _____

   _____

   _____

2.  Abraham sent his servant, Eliezer, to Mesopotamia in order to find a wife for Isaac. Highlight the key points in this narrative by referring to Genesis 24:7, 27, 67. What lessons do you learn?

   _____

   _____

   _____

   _____

   _____

3. In Genesis 26, Isaac received clear instructions from the Lord where to dwell, but unfortunately, he did not obey. List the places where the Lord has instructed you to go—and the places where you shouldn't go.

_____  _____

_____  _____

_____  _____

_____  _____

4. Like Isaac, you can't hear the Lord's voice when you disobey. Read these Scriptures pertaining to obedience and jot down what you discover.

Romans 6:12 _____

2 Thessalonians 3:14 _____

Hebrews 13:17 _____

1 Peter 3:1 _____

5. Some, like Rebekah, have the mistaken notion that God needs our help in accomplishing His work. What was the cost of Rebekah's deception? See Genesis 27:42-45 for help with your answer.

_____

_____

_____

_____

6. The story of Isaac provides us with several intriguing typologies, as Paul reminds us in Galatians 4:28-31. Expound upon how this ministers to you today.

_____

_____

_____

_____

7. When Abraham planned to sacrifice Isaac on the mountain, an angel intervened and spared Isaac's life (Genesis 22:2-12). What did this foreshadow? Why was Isaac's willingness significant?

_____

_____

_____

_____

8. Eliezer's name means, "God, my helper." Read these Scriptures and share how God helps you.

Exodus 18:4 _____

Psalm 40:17 _____

Psalm 121:2 _____

Acts 26:22 _____

9. Genesis portrays Rebekah as a beautiful bride, just as the Lord sees you as His beautiful bride. Examine Psalm 45 and list the characteristics of Christ's bride.

_____ _____

_____ _____

_____ _____

_____ _____

_____ _____

10. God invites you to be His bride. How should you answer the call of God's Spirit?

_____

_____

_____

_____

# Ruth: Adventure of Faith

Read Chapter 10, *Ruth: Adventure of Faith.*

1. At a time of moral decay, religious confusion and outright anarchy, God was still at work. Name the reason why the Lord was working through Naomi's family. Matthew 1:1, 5 may help with your answer.

   _____

   _____

   _____

   _____

2. Read Ruth 1:1-13 and describe the circumstances leading up to Naomi pleading with her daughters-in-law to remain in Moab, their homeland, while she returned to Bethlehem.

   _____

   _____

   _____

   _____

   _____

3. In Ruth 1:16-17, Ruth committed to stay with Naomi as long as she lived. What did her impassioned statement declare?

_____

_____

_____

_____

4. Naomi said, "Do not call me Naomi; call me Mara, for the Almighty has dealt bitterly with me" (Ruth 1:20). How might you keep your heart from bitterness? Read Psalm 64:10 to assist in your response.

_____

_____

_____

_____

5. God was guiding and directing Ruth's steps in ways so natural, she didn't recognize His hand. Reflect on the ways God has guided your steps, even when you didn't know it.

_____

_____

_____

_____

6. Although Ruth was from the pagan country of Moab, Boaz could see that she had come to trust in the true and living God. Look over Ruth 2:5-12 and record the things Boaz admired in her.

_____     _____

_____     _____

_____     _____

_____     _____

_____     _____

7. Deuteronomy 25:5-6 indicates the obligation of the *goel* or kinsman-redeemer. Briefly outline why this law was designed and why each person today needs a Kinsman-Redeemer.

_____

_____

_____

_____

8. Go through the following Scriptures and note your findings about your Kinsman-Redeemer, Jesus Christ.

Job 19:25 _____

Proverbs 23:11 _____

Isaiah 44:6, 24 _____

_____

Colossians 1:14-17 _____

9. The love story of Boaz and Ruth illustrates a beautiful picture of what Jesus did for you on the cross. Write Ephesians 1:7 and inscribe it upon your heart.

_____

_____

_____

_____

10. Your Kinsman-Redeemer is so in love with you—His bride. Write a prayer acknowledging what the Lord has done for you in your adventure of faith.

_____

_____

_____

_____

# Mary: Obedience of Faith

Read Chapter 11, *Mary: Obedience of Faith.*

1. Never underestimate the importance and the power of a godly mother.
   As you ponder this statement, describe the role of a mother in training
   and guiding her children through a life of faith.

   _____

   _____

   _____

   _____

2. God chose Mary and granted her the highest honor of any woman who
   ever lived. Imagine being Mary—being told you would give birth to the
   Savior of the world. In what ways are you inspired by her obedience of
   faith?

   _____

   _____

   _____

   _____

   _____

3. When people object to the idea of the virgin birth, their problem really is with their concept of God. How does Luke 1:37 help you trust in the Lord and walk in obedience to faith?

_____

_____

_____

_____

4. Luke 1:46-55, _The Magnificat_, quotes Mary's glorious exultation to God. Write a sentence or two that reveals Mary's devotion to the Lord.

_____

_____

_____

_____

5. Obedience is not always easy. How did the angel of the Lord strengthen Joseph's faith and encourage him to walk in obedience, according to Matthew 1:20-21?

_____

_____

_____

_____

6. Luke 2:25-32 speaks of a man named Simeon who, because of his faith, was allowed to see the Messiah before he died. Describe Simeon's obedience to faith and what you can glean from it.

_____

_____

_____

_____

7.  When Mary and Joseph found Jesus in the temple, He said, "Why did you seek Me? Did you not know that I must be about My Father's business?" (Luke 2:49). Although Jesus is God Himself, read Luke 2:51 to capture the depth of His statement. Explain the significance.

_____

_____

_____

_____

8.  Jesus' public ministry began when, at the request of His mother, He turned gallons of water into wine. Recall a miracle or something astonishing that the Lord has done in your life which increased your faith.

_____

_____

_____

_____

9.  Mark 3:33-35 says, "Whoever does the will of God is My brother and My sister and mother." How does this minister to you?

_____

_____

_____

_____

10. Mary provides us with a worthy example of a godly disciple of Christ. Read Luke 2:19, 33, 51 and share the importance of Mary's devout mannerisms that reflect her obedience of faith.

_____

_____

_____

_____

# Paul: Apostle of Faith

Read Chapter 12, *Paul: Apostle of Faith.*

1.  Taking a look at Romans 5:1-2, explain the message of grace through faith which Paul preached.

_____

_____

_____

_____

2.  Acts 9:15 reveals that Paul was God's chosen vessel. What was Paul's threefold ministry as described in this verse?

_____

_____

_____

_____

3. The Lord is calling you to share your faith with others. Make a list of people who do not know the Lord as their personal Savior and begin to pray for them daily.

_____   _____

_____   _____

_____   _____

_____   _____

4. Read Galatians 1:15-16. Just as God separated Paul from birth and prepared him for ministry, God also has a specific plan for you. How can your background and past experiences help you to minister to others today?

_____

_____

_____

_____

5. When Paul received the revelation of Jesus Christ, the Lord readjusted his understanding of the Scriptures and the meaning of faith. From these verses, distinguish the work of God that Paul came to realize.

John 6:29 _____

_____

Philippians 3:9 _____

_____

6. God used a humble and willing servant to give specific instructions to Paul and Barnabas for a specific work. From these Scriptures, describe various ways the Lord makes His plans known to you.

Mark 1:2 _____

Luke 12:12 _____

John 14:26 _____

7. In Acts 15, the church council in Jerusalem officially recognized that various men can minister to different groups. Read Ephesians 4:4-6 and expound upon how this changes your view of other Christian churches whose format may be different from where you fellowship.

_____

_____

_____

_____

_____

8. After looking over Philippians 3:4-9, explain why salvation through faith and not of works meant so much to Paul.

_____

_____

_____

_____

9. By your faith and trust in Jesus Christ, God accounts His righteousness to you. List the results of a faith in Jesus Christ, referencing Romans 5:1 and Ephesians 2:8.

_____ _____

_____ _____

_____ _____

_____ _____

10. Paul has taught us to be an apostle of faith—not an apostle of works. Read these Scriptures to clarify this truth further and note your findings.

Romans 4:2 _____

Galatians 2:16 _____

Titus 3:5 _____

# Peter: From Doubt to Faith

Read Chapter 13, *Peter: From Doubt to Faith.*

1.  Can you think of a time when everything seemed to go wrong? What was your reaction to that particular day?

    _____

    _____

    _____

    _____

    _____

2.  We often have a higher opinion of ourselves than is warranted. Instead of comparing ourselves to the world, explore these verses to see what happens when we look at ourselves in light of the presence of God.

Genesis 32:10 _____

Isaiah 6:5 _____

Luke 5:8 _____

3.  After Peter doubted, Jesus brought him to a place of faith. In Luke 5:10, God calls Peter into ministry when he believes Jesus. God has a calling for you too. What is your response?

_____

_____

_____

_____

4.  As you have gone from doubt to faith, share what the Lord's call is for you today. Consider Ephesians 4:1 and write it here.

_____

_____

_____

_____

_____

5.  Like Peter, you may have a tendency to accept logic rather than have faith in God. Read the account in Luke 5:4-9 and note the result of Peter's faith in the Lord—incomparable to his common sense.

_____

_____

_____

_____

6.  When you put your faith in the Lord, He will take away your fears, doubts, and anxieties. Copy the "immediate" words of Jesus from Matthew 14:27 and commit them to memory.

_____

_____

_____

_____

7.  Where you fix your gaze will determine the difference between faith and doubt. Make a list of your concerns and worries today, and pray for the Lord to transform your doubt into faith.

_____     _____

_____     _____

_____     _____

_____     _____

8.  After Peter denied our Lord three times, Jesus did not look at him with disappointment or rebuke but with eyes of love. Read Romans 2:4 and describe what this verse means to you in terms of faith and failure.

_____

_____

_____

_____

9.  Peter's transformation from doubt to faith is highlighted in Acts 3 and 4. Read these Scriptures and emphasize Peter's acts of faith.

Acts 3:1 _____

Acts 3:6-7 _____     _____

Acts 3:12-16 _____

Acts 4:8-13 _____

10. The Lord gave Peter such great faith through the filling of the Holy Spirit—and He can do the same for you. Read Acts 3:19 and establish the refreshing that comes from the presence of the Lord.

_____

_____

_____

_____

# The Soldier & the Mother: Great Faith

Read Chapter 14, *The Soldier & the Mother: Great Faith.*

1.  Peruse Matthew 8:5-13 and Matthew 15:22-28. Describe the only two people Jesus commended for their faith. Does it surprise you that they weren't spiritual leaders or disciples?

    _____

    _____

    _____

    _____

    _____

2.  The Roman centurion showed not only great faith but also great humility—which is what grabs the attention of the Lord. What can be said about you? Read these verses and list how you can display humility to attain great faith.

Romans 12:16 _____

Ephesians 4:2 _____

Philippians 2:3 _____

3. Jesus had interacted with many people, and on occasion had voiced stern words for those who followed Him—but He was amazed at the Roman soldier's faith. Compare the rebuke Jesus gave to His disciples to the blessing He gave to the centurion in Matthew 8:11-13.

_____

_____

_____

_____

4. In contrast to Jesus' recognition of the faith of these two Gentiles, what was the rebuke given to His disciples in the following verses?

Matthew 6:30 _____

Matthew 8:26 _____

Matthew 14:31 _____

5. See Matthew 15:22-28. What were four obstacles the Gentile woman had to overcome in order to demonstrate her great faith to the Lord?

_____

_____

_____

_____

6. At one point this woman cried out to the Lord for help and He said nothing in return. When the Lord is silent towards you, what is your natural reaction? What does that do for your faith? What usually is the outcome of that situation?

_____

_____

_____

_____

7. Sometimes you may become discouraged because you feel unworthy to come to the Lord in prayer. Like this woman, you have the privilege to ask for His mercy. How does Hebrews 4:16 encourage you?

_____

_____

_____

_____

8. The power of persistent or prevailing prayer has a great effect on those around you as it opens the door for the Lord's work to be done—in turn, increasing your faith. Write 1 Thessalonians 5:17-18 and commit it to memory.

_____

_____

_____

_____

9. After studying the great faith of the Roman centurion and the Syro-Phoenician woman, explain how their lives minister to you. What can you learn from them?

_____

_____

_____

_____

10. Write a prayer bringing all of your troubles and worries to the Lord, and go forth rejoicing in the fact that He hears you—whether you receive an immediate answer or not.

_____

_____

_____

_____

# PART THREE

# The Walk of Faith

# Living by Faith in a Faithful God

Read Chapter 15, *Living by Faith in a Faithful God.*

1.  The Lord is faithful and worthy of our trust—even when we lack faith in Him. Copy Joshua's testimony of his faith in God written in Joshua 21:45.

_____

_____

_____

2.  Unfortunately, there are many times when you will be unfaithful to the Lord—yet God has promised that He will always remain faithful despite your faults. Write 2 Timothy 2:13 and imprint its truth upon your heart.

_____

_____

_____

3.  Read Esther chapter 4 and note how Mordecai lived by faith. He believed God's Word would stand whether Esther did or not. List Mordecai's examples on how he lived by faith.

_____      _____

_____      _____

_____      _____

4.  Because you study the Bible, you can live by faith as you continually witness God's faithfulness. Meditate on Isaiah 7:14 and Isaiah 9:6 and note your response to the faithful Word of God.

_____

_____

_____

_____

5.  The faithfulness of God sparks a glorious assurance and a blessed hope to the believer. Read the following verses and state how God's Word will help you live by faith.

Numbers 23:19 _____

Matthew 24:35 _____

Romans 8:28 _____

6.  Galatians 6:7-8 states that a man will sow what he reaps—and God is faithful to His Word. Read Galatians 5:19-23, listing actions produced by living after the flesh and actions born of living by faith.

FLESH                         FAITH

_____      _____

_____      _____

_____      _____

_____      _____

_____      _____

7. Man's word changes constantly, but the Word of God will never change. Survey James' words of encouragement to help you live by faith in a faithful God.

James 1:6 _____

James 1:17 _____

James 1:21 _____

8. God will perform His Word whether you live by faith or not. Read Philippians 4:4-8 and jot down these great rules to help you live by faith.

_____     _____

_____     _____

_____     _____

_____     _____

_____     _____

9. Doubting God's promises leads to depression, but believing God's promises helps you to sing and rejoice. How might you exemplify this to others?

_____

_____

_____

_____

10. To live a life of faith, one must believe the promises of God. By looking at the following Scriptures, write the common truth which reminds you to keep the faith.

Philippians 3:21 _____

2 Timothy 1:12 _____

Hebrews 2:18 _____

# How Can I Pray in Faith?

Read Chapter 16, *How Can I Pray in Faith?*

1. According to James 5:16 what is the result of the fervent prayer of a righteous man? What do you think James means by "avails much"?

_____

_____

_____

_____

2. What is a good definition of an effective, fervent prayer?

_____

_____

_____

_____

_____

3.  Prayer is an essential step in our walk of faith. King David wrote his prayers in the book of Psalms demonstrating to us that we can call out to God at any time and from any place. Glance over Psalm 69:13-15 and record your thoughts.

_____

_____

_____

_____

4.  When you are troubled and have no understanding, what should you do? Research these Scriptures to find your answer.

Psalm 61:1-2 _____

Ecclesiastes 12:13-14 _____

Luke 2:19 _____

5.  After reading Psalm 62:1-2, turn to Psalm 62:6-8 and record how David's perspective changes.

_____

_____

_____

_____

6.  The Lord desires to lift you up out of the miry clay and establish your steps. Examine Psalm 40:1-5 and explain how David's deliverance ministers to you.

_____

_____

_____

_____

7.  We often put God in a box and get stuck following the same pattern rather than seeking God's guidance for every situation. What are some ways you can keep yourself from becoming entrapped in a spiritual rut?

    _____

    _____

    _____

    _____

8.  Consider your actions in the past when you did not take the opportunity to pray or think things through. Write out and memorize Isaiah 40:31 so you can recall it every time you feel rushed and overwhelmed.

    _____

    _____

    _____

    _____

9.  When praying, you wait expectantly to be given an answer. List and describe the three basic kinds of givers. Which giver does God most resemble? Use 2 Chronicles 16:9 and Matthew 6:8 to help with your answer.

    _____

    _____

    _____

    _____

10. Do you believe that God will never leave you to fend for yourself but will help you when you are unsure of what to pray? From Romans 8:26, describe how the Lord helps us to pray in faith.

    _____

    _____

    _____

    _____

# How Can I Step Out in Faith?

Read Chapter 17, *How Can I Step Out in Faith?*

1.  To step out in faith requires wisdom from God. With this in mind, summarize what you learn from James 1:2-6.

_____

_____

_____

_____

_____

2.  Stepping out in faith will become easier when you believe that the Lord is guiding you. Note these verses to further your step.

Psalm 37:23 _____

Proverbs 3:5-6 _____

_____

Proverbs 4:26-27 _____

_____

3. Read Numbers 13:26-33 and 14:1-10. Recap what happened when Joshua and Caleb wanted to step out in faith and enter the Promised Land.

_____

_____

_____

_____

4. Forty years later, when Joshua was finally able to lead the children of Israel into the Promised Land, Caleb once again wanted to step out in faith. What is the wonderful testimony of Caleb given in Joshua 14:14? How does this inspire you?

_____

_____

_____

_____

5. Why do you think so many people are afraid to step out in faith?

_____

_____

_____

_____

6. Looking at 1 Corinthians 1:27, depict the kind of people God desires to use to accomplish His work. Why does He use them?

_____

_____

_____

_____

7.  Satan tries to hinder God's work. What tool does he often use and what is the remedy? Look up the following verses for your answer.

Psalm 23:4 _____

Psalm 118:6 _____

Proverbs 29:25 _____

8.  As noted in 2 Peter 2:5, Noah was a preacher of righteousness and he stepped out in faith by obeying God in building the ark. Contemplate what that must have been like to be ridiculed for 100 years and write your thoughts.

_____

_____

_____

_____

9.  Stepping out in faith does not involve begging others for help. God wants to do the work to glorify Him. Examine what Romans 4:20-21 says about faith and jot down what you find.

_____

_____

_____

_____

10. Has the Lord been speaking to your heart about a work He wants to do through you? Write a prayer of surrender and commitment that you will trust Him to take that step of faith.

_____

_____

_____

_____

# How Can I Stand Firm in Faith?

Read Chapter 18, *How Can I Stand Firm in Faith?*

1.  Despite horrible circumstances, Job's faith in God remained strong. What was his cry in Job 13:15 that testified he was going to stand firm in his faith regardless of his situation?

    _____

    _____

    _____

    _____

2.  Sometimes what we think is a blessing actually turns out to be a curse, and vice versa. Reflect for a moment and share a situation where you found this to be true.

    _____

    _____

    _____

    _____

3. God knows the future and sees the consequences of our actions, determining the lessons we need to learn. Isaiah 55:9 is a fantastic verse to hold on to when we need help standing firm in our faith. Write it here and memorize it.

_____

_____

_____

_____

4. Much like an infant trying to understand complex philosophical questions, we simply cannot understand God's ways because they are infinitely higher than our ways. How does Romans 11:33 amplify this truth?

_____

_____

_____

_____

5. According to Hebrews 11:27, why were the men of faith in the Bible able to stand firm during hard times?

_____

_____

_____

_____

6. Since 2 Peter 1:9 says we have such a difficult time seeing things afar off, how can these Scriptures encourage you to stand firm in your faith?

Romans 8:18 _____

2 Corinthians 4:16-18 _____

_____

1 Peter 5:9 _____

7. Realizing how much the Lord loves us and that He has eternal purposes in mind helps us to stand firm in our faith. What advice does the psalmist give you in Psalm 37:5?

_____

_____

_____

_____

8. The walk of faith at times can seem like a marathon worrying whether or not you have the strength to endure to the end. Research the following verses and record what you learn.

Psalm 138:8 _____

Philippians 1:6 _____

Hebrews 12:2a _____

9. According to Jude 1:21, how can you stand firm in your faith?

_____

_____

_____

_____

10. First Peter 4:19 tells us, "Let those who suffer according to the will of God commit their souls to Him in doing good, as to a faithful Creator." Express your trust in the Lord as your faithful, loving Creator and write a prayer asking Him to help you stand strong despite your hardships.

_____

_____

_____

_____

19

# How Can I Pass Tests of Faith?

Read Chapter 19, *How Can I Pass Tests of Faith?*

1.  God will test your faith to reveal what's really in your heart. Why is it difficult to know the truth about yourself? Find the answer in Jeremiah 17:9-10.

    _____

    _____

    _____

    _____

2.  As Peter explains, we shouldn't be surprised when the genuineness of our faith is tested (1 Peter 4:12). Describe God's promise to you found in Isaiah 43:2 during these tests of faith.

    _____

    _____

    _____

    _____

3. The testing of your faith can also be used to grow and mature your faith. When you see God's faithfulness in the little trials, how does that enable you to pass the really big tests?

_____

_____

_____

_____

4. Write your thoughts about the realization that everyone gets tested—and sometimes retested in certain areas. In what ways does reading this comfort you?

_____

_____

_____

_____

5. God allowed even His only begotten Son to be tested. As stated in Hebrews 4:15, what was the reason for Jesus' testing? Share how this can help you pass tests of faith.

_____

_____

_____

_____

6. Although you may want to complain, James 1:2 exhorts the kind of attitude you should display in times of testing. What does this verse tell you?

_____

_____

_____

_____

7. According to Luke 6:22-23 and 1 Peter 4:12-13, why should you rejoice in a trial?

_____

_____

_____

_____

8. Though tests of faith can be difficult, there is a rewarding result—patience. Copy Romans 5:3 and James 1:3 here and commit them to memory.

_____

_____

_____

_____

9. After reading 1 Peter 1:6-7, explain the spiritual parallel between your trials and the purification process of gold.

_____

_____

_____    _____

_____

10. We want to pass tests of faith that we may not be ashamed at His coming. Create a list of ways you can be made more like the image of Christ so that you will be ready for His return.

_____    _____

_____    _____

_____    _____

_____    _____

_____    _____

# How Can I Grow in Faith?

Read Chapter 20, *How Can I Grow in Faith?*

1. In Luke 17:5 the apostles asked the Lord to increase their faith. Examine this passage and note what prompted the apostles to pray for growth in their faith.

_____

_____

_____

_____

2. Can you recall a time in your life when things looked so desperate, you almost quit? Read Hebrews 13:20-21 to discover who causes your growth and why.

_____

_____

_____

_____

3.  If you observe how some believers live, you are able to see that something is lacking in their faith. Sum up the instructions found in each of these verses.

Proverbs 8:13 _____

Deuteronomy 1:36 _____

Joshua 1:9 _____

Philippians 4:6 _____

4.  The Lord said concerning Paul, "He is a chosen vessel of Mine, and I will show him how many things he must suffer for My sake" (Acts 9:15-16). Note from Romans 8:18 Paul's response to his sufferings.

_____

_____

_____

_____

5.  Referring to 1 Thessalonians 3:10, what is one route through which you can grow in your faith?

_____

_____

_____

_____

6.  Another way you can grow in your faith is through continual interaction and fellowship with other Christians. Write out Proverbs 27:17 and jot down how you can incorporate it in your life today.

_____

_____

_____

_____

7. Reflect on the examples found in Hebrews 11. What can you glean from the faith of these Old Testament men and women?

_____

_____

_____

_____

8. The more time you spend in the Word, the more your faith will be perfected. Record what you extract from these Scriptures.

Isaiah 55:11 _____

Romans 10:17 _____

1 Peter 1:23 _____

9. Take an inventory of your thoughts and actions over the past week. Do you need a stronger faith? Summarize several ways you have learned from this chapter in which your faith can grow, and give practical steps to appropriate them.

_____

_____

_____

_____

10. God uses ordinary people to serve Him because they have little interest in bringing glory to themselves. How can your faith bring glory to God?

_____

_____

_____

_____